The blood of
Darkness ru
veins. . .

2♡

ANIMA

~~Duende~~
Goblin
Queen

Mystery.

Yet Pupa Bones IS the Devil.

Is MY Devil.

Samael being my father,
the Objective Devil

Obeah: A Sorcerous Ossuary

OBEAH: A SORCEROUS OSSUARY
Text Copyright © 2013 Nicholaj de Mattos Frisvold
Cover Art Copyright © 2013 Kyle Fite
All Rights Reserved Worldwide.
Published by Hadean Press
Printed in Great Britain

ISBN 978 1 907881 37 4

Obeah
A Sorcerous Ossuary

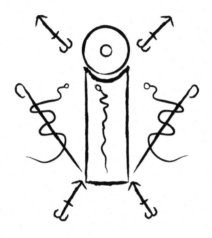

Nicholaj de Mattos Frisvold

HADEAN

CONTENTS

FOREWORD

OBEAH IS A SORCEROUS CULT, A PERSONAL AND UNIQUE ART rooted in spirit pacts and spirit trafficking—as such it is difficult to explain its tenets in a uniform way. It is difficult to explain because sorcery tends to be highly pragmatic in its orientation, and thus is centered on one's merging and induction to a spirit patron or patrons that support the sorcerous power and teach the sorcerer in the virtues of that power. I believe sorcery is indicative of what is hidden in the Latin word, *sortiarius*, 'someone who can influence the Fates by manipulating lots'. These lots are pieces of fortune, fragments of reality that can be worked in a great variety of ways. It also suggests that the sorcerer has access to spiritual powers that can thwart Fate.

Like many sorcerous traditions, Obeah takes its power from the woods and sees trees and bushes as arcane spirits. By working the realm of the Lord of the Woods, Sasabonsam, we work with spirits old and wise, spirits saturated in magical cunning. Obeah has, by scholars and adventurers, been described as animism and fetishism. To the extent that everything mineral, vegetal and animal possesses a soul we can agree to the animist label—and it follows that fetishism, the use of external objects endowed with a particular soul and the work of this soul for a given purpose, is also true.

To give a systematic account of Obeah is not only difficult, but it would defy the nature of the tradition. At the core of the tradition is found *obiya* or *sasa*, a natural power that can facilitate transformation. The obiya is just this, a power *given*—an amoral power that transforms.

I was introduced to Obeah more than two decades ago by a man from Trinidad. He was a Sango Baptist and also an Obeahman. He described to me how his initiation to Obeah was like a dark fairytale, an encounter with the devil. He tried to scare me away and introduced me to a spiritual form of Sango Baptism that he thought suitable for me. During this spiritual training I had my own encounter with the devil and learned that his name was Papa Bones, also called 'The Lord of Darkness'.

After this I was formally given the obiya and we started to work together, as well as with his 'shamanic' study group. Each shamanic session began with our solitary communion with Papa Bones and his guardian, Anima Sola; the sacrificial offering was apricot brandy or one of its varieties veiled in the fumes of tobacco. The work we did together was astonishing and much healing was accomplished.

In this period I still had difficulties understanding the simple mechanism at play that made this potential for healing possible. I expected to be taught some sort of doctrine or system, but I was not taught either—I was simply given a power by a pact with spirit, and it was this power that gave what was needed to accomplish our work. So, to give a descriptive and analytical presentation of a system when we speak of Obeah is simply not possible as it will defy its pragmatic force and orientation. Obeah is a force that acts upon something in conformity with how it is directed.

What is possible to give is a conglomerate of texts and rituals that speak of what Obeah is, and such is my intention with this monograph. I have become aware over the years that Obeah is not a term unique to what was transmitted to me, but a force of resonance that can take varied shapes and forms. For instance in Jamaica, Obeahmen tends to dress in red and cultivate a sinister image, whilst in Trinidad they seek the refuge of *Sasabonsam*, the protective spirit of the woods.

Given the dynamic implicit in inheriting a force by virtue of a pact, the deep mystery at times gets lost when one seeks to integrate Obeah into a system or to make a syncretism. It is not like that; Obeah is a *primum mobile* that ensorcells the Obeah man in such a way that what the Obeah man does is Obeah—but this calls for a clarity of perspective, an awareness of what one is doing and why and with the aid of whom.

For the sake of clarity: Obeah has much in common with the work of *djabs* in Haiti or the relationship with the demons of 'Lemegeton' that is established because one makes a pact with a spirit king—or even what happens when a Sufi establishes his or her relationship with the Qarinah. It is a unique relationship that transcends any attempt of systematization. It is a pact that provides dynamic interaction with the secrets of Fate. The spirit of the pact as it concerns Obeah however is Papa Bones—and this pact can only be given by human intervention. As such, we speak of succession and lineage. This monograph is as such fruit given from this particular Trinidadian lineage.

CHAPTER I

VARIETIES OF OBEAH

OBEAH IS NOTORIOUSLY DIFFICULT TO DEFINE FOR THOSE searching for a coherent system abiding by this name. Obeah is, like witchcraft, a sorcerous art exercised by the one who possesses the 'obi'—or power. The Obeahman or woman inherits a particular power that aids effectively in enhancing the potency of their spellcraft, duppy-catching and sorcery.

A common mistake seen in referencing Obeah is that it is often presented as a unified practice, a system. This is largely caused by Obeah entering the Western consciousness with the writings of Joseph J. Williams' *Voodoos and Obeahs* (1925) and Hesketh Bells' *Obeah* (1889). Both books are worthy as they give intimate and lively narratives of Obeah—and they leave the reader with a plethora of what Obeah might be, much of it quite accurate. Another element that gives the idea that Obeah was a unified cult was the fact that its practice was prohibited by law in large parts of the Caribbean up until quite recently. These laws basically replicated the content of European 'witchcraft laws', which would suggest that the colonizers saw Obeah as a form of witchcraft.

As for myself, I was initiated by an Obeahman from Trinidad in the early 1990s and when I met him I also held this belief, that Obeah was a unified sorcerer's cult.

This belief was soon enough dismantled and buried in favor of direct encounters with the powers of Obeah. Obeah is a power given to understand, and not a system to be taught. If any reference to other African and Afro-diasporic faiths can be made I would say it is like being given *ndoki*, a power ruled by a spiritual intelligence. It can also hold some similarities with receiving a *Makaya djab*—but without the often demanding protocol that comes with such a pact; rather the pact-making with spirits and *djab*-like entities is an integral part of Obeah that is made possible by possessing the power known as Obeah. This spiritual simplicity lies at the heart of Obeah and rather than being the source for a system, it will serve as a nucleus for generating a sorcerous practice given from the merging with this power. Hence the varieties and all seeming confusion in defining Obeah are caused by this fundamental important truth. Over the years I have seen people suggesting Obeah to be a form of witchcraft, and it does hold great similarities with traditional verdant paths of the Witches' craft as given, understood and used. This also goes for Obeah being an initiatic succession; the power is inherited from Obeahman/woman from the previous and given to the next. Hence, there is a widespread belief that the Obeahman passing on his *obi* loses some of his power in favor of him or her who is given this power. This generates carefulness with who is taken into the sorcerous circle and it speaks volumes of the bond generated between the Obeahman and his novice.

A well known Obeah quotation in modern magical circles is from *Liber Al vel Legis*, or *The Book of the Law*, a prophetic text channeled by Aleister Crowley and his wife Rose Edith Kelly in 1904, that mentions the '*obeah and the wanga*' (Al 1: 37)–and in fact how obeah is presented in this text as something similar to wanga is quite correct and replicates the ideas set forth by Bell in his earlier work. It is the power of Obeah that makes a wanga (hex/working) possible; it is the energy of possibility, the tower of power that flashes out to all corners of the world.

This fundamental principle concerning the nature of Obeah being established, it will serve us well to investigate further some accounts of the practice of Obeah in the Caribbean and see if it is possible to trace this practice to an African root.

Obeah has been, since the late 17th Century, used as a loose reference for whatever magical and supernatural work the Africans were doing. Poisonings and healings, as well as any form of spirit work and charms, were understood as obeah. It is important to keep in mind that in the Caribbean the boundaries between orthodoxy, religion and spirituality have always been very flexible, leading to certain practices becoming crystallized into specific concepts through laws and legislations. One example is found with the *Shouters* in Trinidad and Tobago, who were prohibited in 1917. Accusations of obeah, as well as being politically dangerous, surfaced as themes in nearly all processes up to the prohibition being dissolved in 1952. The people called Shouters rarely identified with this label; rather they defined themselves as Spiritual Baptists.

The first account of the African sorceries in the Caribbean was written by Jean-Baptiste Labat and was called *Nouveau Voyage aux Isles de l'Amerique*, published in 1722. In this work he discusses the '*sorcellerie*' of the African slaves, which is basically any form of sorcery, malefica, benefica, and poisoning. This book set a sort of standard and was followed by Edward Long's *History of Jamaica* in 1774, Bryan Edwards's *History of the West Indies* in 1793 and Moreau de Saint-Méry's topographic account of Saint-Domingue in 1797. It is from these works the generalized African 'sorcellerie' was referred to as Obeah, Myalism and Vaudoux. Attempts at distinction were made but the labels tended to blend and fuse in such way that any one of the terms referred back to any of the others.

In the case of Trinidad and Tobago we should also keep in mind the significant Indian and Muslim population, and also how several '*hindoo doctors*' and Muslims were charged with accusations of 'Obeah', whilst their practices were from other parts of this 'cross-oceanic dialogue', as Diana Paton defines it in *Obeah and Other Powers* (2012). We are clearly speaking of a cultural conglomerate of sorcerous practice that can express itself from a common core in a great variety of ways. As we see in present day Trinidad and Tobago, the spiritual landscape is one of heterodoxy and even in the Sango cult we find practices originally coming from Hindus and Muslims being incorporated by synthesis. If we add to this Winti, Zionist movements, and a host of practices understood to be witchcraft/*brujeria* we get an idea of the difficulty in defining Obeah with precision. Nevertheless, we can define its core.

It should also be mentioned that Obeah was perhaps popularized to the greater French-speaking world by Victor Hugo in his short novel called *Bug-Jargal* published in 1826. In this ghostly tale obeah or *obi* is associated with a radical and extreme sorcerous potency. We find obeah at the focus of poisonings, inexplicable deaths of slave owners, barrenness of plantations, and general misfortune. Hugo was most likely taken in with the story about the wave of poisonings and inexplicable deaths that took place in Martinique in the years between 1815 and 1830. During this time the island saw an epidemic of contagious disease, similar to cholera and arsenic poisoning. This wave of disease was blamed solely on a society of black magicians or Obeahmen. Curiously, this epidemic began at the time of Napoleon Bonaparte's Hundred Days in 1815, during which he abolished the slave trade in all French colonies. From 1815 onwards, illness swept through Martinique— an illness that actually affected in greater proportion the African descendants than it did the colonizers. It appears that this was an attempt to clean up the colony, to weed out undesired individuals on a large scale—and that the connotation with Obeah did hold some truth. We can only speculate about the reasons, but one suggestion is that this wave of poisonings was a tactic for getting rid of Christian syncretism and restoring a more pure African spirituality. I don't think it is possible to arrive at any plausible hypothesis about this, but what can be said is that already in the early 18th century syncretism was going deep as the following quotation demonstrates:

> In addition to African mysticism, enlightened reformers often saw the influence of Catholicism as contributing to the superstitious beliefs of the enslaved. The records of a 1755 trial in Martinique for example, detailed the composition of the amulets worn by slaves, which included "incense and holy water, small crucifixes and...almost always holy bread from Christmas or another holy day, and wax from the great Easter candle. (Paton & Forde, 2012: 161).

On a personal level I feel such practices fit quite well in the practice of an Obeahman, as we can see the use of Christian relics and holy items both as a submission to the god of the colonizers and also as a way of taking back the power of their God and using it for personal gain.

The most important realm for the Obeahmen and women is however the woods. The wortcunning of the Africans and Creoles was famed and dreaded, as the "Pharmacopée Noire" fuses the use of plants for medicine and poisoning with a magical dimension that is impossible to separate from the use of plants. And it is here the greatest obi of the Obeahman is found as we will see in the subsequent chapter.

The Jamaican Obeah Law of 1898 targeted those who pretended to possess any supernatural powers and to use these powers for gain. In this time we see that Obeah is referred to as a form of worship, a cult, and a society, but also as a practice and a form of sorcery done by individuals lacking connection to any society. The practices of Obeahmen were, besides poisoning, to a great extent about '*duppy catching*' and the manufacturing of 'hexes'. It was multi-stranded and pragmatic—a practice developed by sorcerers on the move with a keen sense of how to use nature and the spirit world to their advantage.

Some of the practices recurring most in the tracts and texts we have about Obeah are as follows:

- Nailing shadows to the cotton tree in order to effectuate healing
- The manufacturing of hex bottles that are commonly planted at doorsteps

- The nailing of duppies (ghosts and wood spirits) to various trees
- Making workings and powders for influencing court cases
- Love philters
- Manufacturing the 'hand of glory' following '*Le Petit Albert*'

A curious remedy called *Zarouba* should also be mentioned. Zarouba was marketed in several Caribbean islands as a '*miracle philter*', but was in reality blood medicine. It was simply a blood-based infusion manufactured on the idea that blood as pertaining to different species, both man and animal, held distinct properties that held great benefits not only for health, but also for one's 'psychic powers'. This blood gnosis was quite popular for some time and is still a teaching passed on by some Obeahmen. The basic principle is that specific forms of blood hold a given quality that together with carefully selected plant material will produce a particular charm or hex that can be drunk or used in the form of libation on a fetish or any form of working. Williams says about this in *Voodoos and Obeahs*:

> Obeah men are the oldest and most artful Negroes; a peculiarity marks them, and every Negro pays the greatest respect to them, they are perfectly well acquainted with medicinal herbs, and know the poisonous ones, which they often use. To prepossess the stranger in favor of their skill, he is told that they can restore the dead to life; for this purpose he is shown a Negro apparently dead, who, by dint of their art, soon

recovers; this is produced by administering the narcotic juice of vegetables. On searching one of the Obeah men's houses, was found many bags filled with parts of animals, vegetables, and earth, which the Negroes who attended at the sight of, were struck with terror, and begged that they might be christened, which was done, and the impression was done away. In consequence of the rebellion of the Negroes in the year 1760, a Law was enacted that year to render the practice of Obiah, death. (p. 117)

And indeed, the year 1760 was the year when Obeah was considered an offense punishable by death in Jamaica. The law was triggered by subordination from Koromantyn (Ashanti) slaves, but the term obeah was inferred on all African practices and upon people from any African nation.

We find today two main theories explaining the African origin of Obeah. The one that appears to have the greatest precedence currently is that Obeah is from the Igbo people in present day Nigeria. Here we find the traditional practice called *obia*, which is a form of spiritual medicine resorting greatly to the Green Kingdom. These specialists were called *Ndi Obia* and were famous for their manufacture of charms and hexes. The original faith amongst the Igbo is known as *Odinani*, which we can understand to mean 'customs of the land'—*land* in a specific geographical sense. As such, Odinani presents a classical West African cosmological theology where the specific land brings into being the customs needed to reach fulfilment in life by living in harmony and understanding with the land and nature.

The other theory, which ties in with the death penalty given to the practice of Obeah targeting the Ashanti states, is that the Efik word *ubio*, meaning 'ominous', is the origin of Obeah. This practice was relegated by the *Obayifo*, an Akan (Suriname and Guyana) term referring to witchcraft and to those who practice it. We find this heritage well and alive in the practice of Winti and Wisi up to present day. There is naturally nothing wrong in both theories being equally right; the Igbo, Akan and Ashanti saw these similarities themselves and gravitated towards each other by commonality in their captivity. After all, their cosmology and theology are fairly similar—this might have caused a merging of the heritage from their lands replanted in captivity. My initiator however claimed Ashanti pedigree, so I have chosen to stay with this. This being said, the similarities with Odinani faith are numerous.

It is pertinent at this point to look at the cosmology of the Koromantyn people that are basically Ashanti—this people have their roots amongst the Akan—who used to be an enormous kingdom with great influence all over Africa by virtue of their metallurgic skills, especially with works of brass and bronze. It is perhaps through the brass and bronze we find a connection as far Southwest as amongst the Igbo and Yoruba.

The Koromantyn people believed in *Accompong*, which they saw as a distant creator God in conformity with the 'via negativa'. Accompong was identical to the Akan *Nyame*, 'he who doesn't speak'. They did not erect any shrines to Accompong, but praised him in songs and prayers. They did however make cult to *Assarci*, whom they saw as the God of Earth. The Akan knew Assarci as *Anansi*, 'the spider'—this deity ventured to the Caribbean under

the name Anansi, in conformity with his Akan disposition
where he was the teller of tall tales and disperser of wisdom.
Anansi was understood to be the memory of creation—the
mind of Nyame/Accompong, and hence 'spider stories'
were stories that passed on divine wisdom.

The Akan worshipped numerous *obosom*—lesser gods,
if you will—sons and daughters of Nyame. These obosom
were created by a gathering of herbs, sacred items and
stones placed in vessels of brass. Summoned by bells,
chants, dance, and blood, they were given life. The rituals
that invigorated the obosom were called *akomfo*, which was
a dance that gave way to trance and spirit possession. Those
presiding over this dance and rite were called *okomfo* and
were considered the priesthood of the regular order of faith
and mystery. Then we also had the *obayifo*—also known as
obi okomfo—understood to be a wizard. The obayifo were
also known as *Bonsam komfo*, someone who manufactured
suman/charms. These wizards were seen as votaries of
Sasabonsam and their trade and practice was known as
obayi, which was understood to be works connected to the
owner of the greenwood, Sasabonsam, the spider-mind
of God, Anansi, vampirism and works with any hostile
spirits. These hostile spirits in the Caribbean are known
as duppies, which are understood to be like the Vodou
zombie. But before going more deeply into this, let us have
a look at the vital parts as presented in Williams' treatise,
which harmonizes with oral tradition.

From Williams' work we find that the term Obeah is
understood to be derived from the Ashanti Obayifo and
we find a proverb to go with this:

Sasabonsam ko ayi a, osoe obayifo fi a, which means: "when Sasabonsam goes to attend a funeral, he lodges at a witch's house. (p. 130)

Sasabonsam is usually translated as 'devil' and is the particular spirit with which the Obayifo has made a pact. The negative connotation is further stressed by people under the influence of malefic forces being said to carry a *'sesa'* or *'sasa'*. Williams says about Sasabonsam that:

The Sasabonsam of the Gold Coast and Ashanti is a monster which is said to inhabit parts of the dense virgin forests. It is covered with long hair, has large blood-shot eyes, long legs, and feet pointing both ways. It sits on high branches of an odum or onyina tree and dangles its legs, with which at times it hooks up the unwary hunter. It is hostile to man, and is supposed to be essentially at enmity with the real priestly class. Hunters who go to the forest and are never heard of again—as sometimes happens—are supposed to have been caught by Sasabonsam. All of them are in league with abayifo (witches), and with the mmotia (troubling spirits), in other words, with the workers in black magic. As we have seen, however, and will see again farther on, their power is sometimes solicited to add power to the suman (fetish), not necessarily with a view to employing that power for purposes of witchcraft, but rather the reverse. (p. 131)

This passage is interesting because here Williams is actually defining the nucleolus of the cult as 'The Lord of the Forest'. If we turn to Brazil we find this role occupied by *Curupira*. Curupira is at times seen as a midget and other times as a giant with fire for hair and backwards feet. He walks in league with the *caipoiras*, midget spirits who take offerings of alcohol and tobacco and who punish people who abuse nature and hunters that take more than what they need. In Brazil there is also the connotation of someone being followed by a *caipora*, which refers to someone followed by bad luck, thus hearkening back to the essence of 'sasa'. If we turn to the Yoruba people we find the spirit *Osanyin* flanked by his helper, the dogface midget *Aroni*, as the Lord of the Woods. Osanyin is also related to bad luck in several of his stories and holds a fondness for alcohol and tobacco. His fondness for alcohol is so grave that we find drunkards being understood to be under the spell of Osanyin or Aroni in Yorubaland.

As we see, the name Sasabonsam is an amalgam of several words and is in its own right a word of power that can be used to call upon his presence in various permutations. Sasa denotes a particular power, while *saman* is usually understood to be a ghostly apparition. This word is never used to define anything natural or human—it holds a complete and distinct supernatural meaning; it is something external that can be given or encountered. The sasa on the other hand is a part of the human soul, the part that can shift shape and fly out—hence it is often judged as a negative part of the soul. Sasa is also associated with the 'duppies', which are considered to be both ghosts and nature spirits or fairies. It does however seem that the sasa is a form of the active and transformative agent of the soul, as it is the sasa that is laid to rest during funerals. In the activities of shadow-catching and shadow-nailing it is the sasa that is caught and nailed.

As for the nature of Obeah, Williams summarises it as follows:

> And so it came to pass that Obeah did in a sense develop more and more as a religion in which, of course, the object of worship was not the Divine Being but rather the evil spirit whether we refer to him as Sasabonsam or Obboney, and whom we must regard either as the Evil One, or perhaps more properly one of his satellites. The act of worship, however, is not really one of adoration, but pacification or propitiation, wherein an effort is made to assuage his enmity and restrain his vindictiveness. (p. 201)

This is a fairly accurate summary as this entire terminology and understanding of Sasabonsam is still intact amongst Obeahmen in Trinidad and Tobago—and I assume in Jamaica. So from this a sort of Obeah cosmology can be presented.

At the root we find sasa, which is similar to the Akan concept of *kra*, denoting the part of the soul that 'flies out'. It is this potency Sasabonsam embodies. In addition to this active part of the soul we have the saman and mmoatia which are spirits holding troubling potential. It was these spirits that became known as duppies in the Caribbean.

The part of the soul that is animated and animates is known as *sunsum*—and everything that is possesses sunsum; hence we find here the cause for what the colonizers called animism—that everything is ensouled. A particular form of sunsum was found in *samanfo*, ancestral spirits which Ashanti kings had to drink as they took their royal power. This drink was an herbal infusion mixed with alcohol that would leave the king in a state of trance where the memory of ancestry would flow into him. By this act the king would become Oto, a King Zombie. But the idea of a Zombie was far from what we see in popular imagination. Rather a zombie was someone who had been subject to possession by his or her samanfo. These forms of possession are moved by the zombie spirit *Macoo*, who in the more Christian-oriented '*cuminas*' (possession dance) is said to have facilitated possession with biblical prophets. Cumina, from the Kimbundu 'to see through', in reference to clairvoyance and the eyes that open in trance, was a funeral celebration with its attending necromantic mysteries. They were also doing *cumama*, 'to call the Dead mother', a reference to the Mother of the Pitch Lake. This was probably a fusion of Arawak and Kimbundu practices.

Through such possession a form of ancestry is then laid down and re-forged; because of this, the divine consciousness—and by extension ancestry—is understood to be like a spider web.

Tales of the gods are called *Anansesem*—spider stories. These stories, as well as gossip and the like, can only be told when the Moon is up and preferably full, because she delights in such matters and will never tell God about them. Anansi/Anansy is the active part of the divine consciousness and is seen as a spider god, a washer of souls and a trickster. On this web the *Abosomakotere* (chameleon) walks.

Myalism is considered to be a form of white magic countering the Obeah, probably from the Hausa word *maye*, 'evil' and *le*, 'to take'. The practitioners appear to have been zealous adherents of the official Ashanti faith and thus they waged war on Obeah because they were Obeahmen themselves, but wished to uphold the official cult. They also incorporated a ritual of vigil lasting nine days and are recorded to have used Loyola's *Spiritual Exercises* for initiatic purposes, suggesting that some Christian-rooted contempt for obeah, understood as witchcraft, also played a role in the Myalist attempts of eradicating Obeah.

The contemporary situation is however quite different. We might see Obeah as a thaumaturgical cult freestanding on the point of Sasabonsam, but it has also become integrated with the social and accepted forms of religiosity—at least to some extent—both for the Sango cult and the Spiritual Baptists.

We can find an organization of Obeah similar to what we find in Suriname's Winti faith. Here we find a variety of offices that one can hold in the cult, some of them being *Rut mang*, which is a herbalist and healer, *Luku mang* which is a diviner, *Obia mang*, which is a priestly magician who knows the secrets of the woods and *Wisi mang*, which is the exorcist who has specialized knowledge about harmful magic. In this context Oby/Obia is seen as a particular form of power of which both the Obia mang and Wisi mang know the secrets.

This secret is frequently said to be held by The Prince of Darkness—a clear reference to Sasabonsam, mediated through a Christian lens. The understanding however is not Christian, because even if The Prince of Darkness knows the secret of evil and darkness it doesn't mean that he is evil incarnate, as the Obia mang and Wisi mang are not automatically evil because of the wisdom they possess. Rather, The Prince of Darkness represents the knowledge of turbulence and radical change in the world—and because of this he can be a source for great stability.

CHAPTER II

AFRO-SHAMANIC WITCHCRAFT

AS SEEN IN THE PREVIOUS CHAPTER, OBEAH DOES NOT REFER
to a given system, but a sorcerous trade. Since there is no
definition for the system, it is has been constantly difficult
for Westerners and their preoccupation with taxonomy
and categories. So, Obeah has been described as a form of
Vodou, as sorcery, as witchcraft and as any criminal activity
with the aid of supernatural powers in the Caribbean.
The attempts at defining its origin are as confused as is
defining its nature and this is most proper for what Obeah
is, because it is 'a tower of power'—a storehouse or occult
engine of supernatural power owned by Papa Bones and
gifted to his votaries.

Williams and Bell both suggested that Obeah held
some connection with the Witch of Endor and her
practice of Ob, as well as the python veneration found
in Dahomey and Ouidah—and indeed the yellow python
is seen by some as sacred to Papa Bones, a vehicle of his
sasa, or power. From island to island Obeah is understood
slightly differently in terms of practice, but there are a few
common elements. If it be in St. Vincent, Trinidad, Tobago
or Jamaica, Obeah constantly holds a connotation with
red and dangerous spirits of the woods, hence the most
common association with Obeahmen as being herbalists
and spirit workers. Their sources of power are, however,

volatile and dangerous powers of the night, and it is not uncommon to hear them say that they gained their powers from 'the Devil' or 'The Prince of Darkness/Evil'.

When it comes to the sorcerous technology of Obeah it is highly pragmatic. Some might say it is eclectic— but I have my reservations with this. We might see the Obeahman as the icon of the Chaos magician as he enters realities and bends the world in conformity with the possibilities inherited in his powers. Whilst the Chaos magician is eclectic and psychological in his work with the paradigms in the manifested world, the Obeahman works the layers in pragmatic ways, making reality possible from a spiritual point of reference, the source of his powers. So, even if an Obeahman can be seen as working with Kali Ma side by side with nailing shadows to trees and making herbal infusions worthy of any alchemist or rootworker, this is not in any way an eclectic practice—it is a pragmatic one. The idea is that whatever tool, spell or rite the Obeahman infuses with his 'obi' will, for the duration of use, be a form of Obeah—this does *not* mean that the Obeahman is generating a religious system around his practice. The only rituals and works I have seen repeating themselves as a type of core ritual are those for Papa Bones and Anima Sola, who holds and moves the 'obi'. As for the rest it is a dance in the lands of possibility and chance where the end justifies the means, but even here we find a commonality in the use of herbs, minerals, animal parts and chants to effectuate change and bring on the desired results.

In Trinidad and Tobago, Obeah may or may not be found amongst the 'Spiritual Baptist' and the 'Baptist Orisa'—and at times amongst the 'Sango'. In my case, my mentor was a 'Baptist' both Spiritual and Orisa and for him Obeah was just a station on his path towards being a 'Baptist Shepherd'. Even though Obeah was found amongst these religions it was not an integral part of them, but a path acknowledged that some should pursue for various reasons. Obeah is considered to be a power needed in the world, a natural power guarded by red-hot spirits of the night and the initiation is always conferred by 'the devil' taking hold of the Obeahman so this fire can be transmitted to the acolyte. This means that Obeah is actually initiatic and hence the reference in the annals of history describing Obeahmen as a being composed of a 'guild' is not far from the truth.

Obeah differs from witchcraft, where one can be born with this particular potency. Obeah is a power inherited, and thus all Obeahmen make part of a succession of this inheritance, this particular sasa. This sasa gives to the Obeahman the power to awaken the spirit of plants and bones; it gives the power of night-hunt and domination over spirits, especially the duppies black, red and white. In this we find Obeah to be 'shamanic' in nature as it is about spirit traffic and domination of the invisible realm, but we also find the power of night-stalking and skin-leaping here. Potentiality resting in the sasa of the Obeahman, but given to the Obeahman himself to unbridle. In truth, the sasa is a riddle written in fire and embers and injected into your bloodstream as you become 'obi'. It is the presence of this 'obi' that is detected by Sasabonsam and Papa Bones and constitutes a bond akin to a pact. Those in possession of obi/obiya or those called to receive it are understood to be people often of bad luck that have been called to a narrow road of loneliness and darkness.

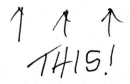

The patron and protector of Obeah is known as Papa Bones. We also have in the Caribbean the wood spirit, Papa Bois, the two having been suggested as being identical with one another. Papa Bois is understood to be a protector and helper of the spirits of the wood. He is an old spirit carrying around his bamboo horn and bamboo sticks. In fact, he is the spirit of the bamboo and is a great shapeshifter and can turn himself into any animal he pleases, but favors stag and wild hog. Papa Bois/Papa Wood is also a quite helpful spirit and is said to help men and animals in trouble in the woods—whilst bringing terrible catastrophes upon those that anger him. In this way he holds more the function of pathfinder and guide than does Papa Bones.

Oral tradition tells that Papa Bones was married to 'the woman in the lake of Pitch'. The Pitch Lake is found in La Brea, southwest of Trinidad. The woman in the pitch lake has been called several things, amongst them *Cumama* and *Asase*. Asase/Asasa is the Ashanti mother of Ananse and owner of earth; her name would suggest that she is the source for the Obeahman's sasa. Cumama holds similar association as it refers to earth and her blackness. The mother of the pitch lake is perhaps, more than anything, considered a form of Kali. This form of Kali is akin to Tripur Bhairavi and Dhumavati—the more destructive and saturnine aspects—or mahavidyas/great wisdoms of Kali-Ma. In particular, the form of Dhumavati where she is propitiated as a large black rock with hungry bloodshot eyes and bleeding mouth would serve well as an icon for the mother of the Pitch Lake. There is clearly an interesting transition here where Tripur Bhairavi represents the becoming of the mother of the Lake of Pitch, while

Bhairavi *is* the lake. The symbol and what it represents has merged into a unity of mutual reference. Tradition imparts that the daughter of the Pitch Lake was Anima Sola; hence the Christian icon of St. Anthony of Padua holding a child is at times seen as Papa Bones holding Anima Sola. In Palo Mayombe, St. Anthony is known as *Cuye Lumbembe*, a sorcerer-priest born from thunder and lightning (Nsasi), not much different from St. Cyprian.

I can testify to Cuye Lumbembe and Papa Bones sharing a distinct commonality, which has led me to embrace St. Anthony of Padua as a proper icon for him. Another icon used is St. Expedite, given because of his speed in effectuating workings, but also his association with crows and the period of the daily cycle ruled by crows—namely from twilight to twilight.

The path of Papa Bones is not for everyone. It holds
a certain allure in its promise of power, but possessing the
obiya comes with a price and this price is related to the
knowledge of death. It might be because of this 'knowledge
of death' some Obeahmen found it opportune to work
with Loyola's Spiritual Exercises as a way of understanding
the complexities of this mystery, especially those parts of
Loyola's Christology focusing on the mystery of passion,
death and resurrection. Possession of the 'knowledge
of death' tends to impair—at least for some time until it
balances out—one's happiness. Consequently a large part
of Obeahmen and women have chosen lives as recluses,
while others have chosen a more active trade as sorcerers-
for-hire. Possession of obiya mediates between these two
extremes, as a certain misanthropy is bound to take hold
of the Obeahman. The access offered to the wisdom of
existence and how to change it relies on the practitioner's
ability to recognize his or her own heart of hearts in a
manner that draws proper cells of attunement close to the
practitioner's knowledge of Self in the light of Death. The
path of Papa Bones is lethal in the way that he gives his
children tools and formulas of a direct and instant power
that infuses them with the ability to severely destroy and
alter whatever comes in the Obeahman's path.

Caused by all these associations with death, the
passion of Christ and Crucifixion, Papa Bones has been
syncretised with Satan and holds as epitaphs The Prince of
Darkness/The Prince of Evil/The Prince of Hell. The fact
that Obeahmen gravitate toward grammars of the 'black
arts' and their practice, which is often known as 'working
the kabbalah' has certainly contributed to this association.
Obeahmen tend to be amused by this association, because

in a way it is true, but they also hold that Papa Bones is more like Moses than the biblical Satan. Satan in the cosmological vision of the Obeahman represents the power of exorcism and the 'knowledge of Death'. The knowledge of Death represents the total knowledge of existence and therefore this knowledge is what constitutes the obiya and gives the power of transformation to the Obeahman.

From the texts of Labat, Bell and Williams we find Obeah being related somehow to 'voudaux'—a term they used to try to pinpoint something Africanesque happening in the Caribbean. But in truth there is an uncanny resemblance between the Ghuede Lwa and Papa Bones. I was told that Papa Bones was himself the jawbone of the skull and therefore the oracular essence: the Bone that speaks. But all bones in the body represent his legions and all these bones hold a pact with trees and bushes. Considering that Sasabonsam, the Lord of the Woods, is the source for obiya, Papa Bones is the force that disperses and administrates this power to humans by fusing the very skeleton with the powers of Sasabonsam. In this he is indeed very much like Roi Ghuede as we meet him in Vodou—and even the mystery, 'the knowledge of Death' binds then close together. We see this by the way he appears to his votaries in dream, often as a dancing skeleton or as a bald man, usually brown of hue, with flashing yellow/golden eyes. In this form he represents the trees and arbours as they flash in spiritual vitality. He is a serious spirit and quite void of the vulgarism and humour we find with the Ghuede. He is clearly a mystery of Death and as such the vitalisation of the Obeahman and woman's bones will be saturated with an erotic pulse— because *eros* knows death as much as life...

Sasabonsam himself is depicted as the monstrous Lord of the Forest, a demonic 'Green Man' that hides amongst leaves and branches of the thick forest and walks with the creatures of the night. Sasabonsam is reputed to assault people wandering alone in the forest and consume their vitality and blood. In Jamaica this deity became associated with the "Bogieman", the creature that hides under children's bed at night waiting to eat them.

Obeah is very pragmatic in how it selects its tools. Its vastness allows it to handle a wide range of sorcerous technologies that are then fused with this dramatic power of obiya. The spirit of trees, plants and animals who have the woods as their home are the natural tutors for the Obeahman. So, Obeah is not eclectic in any way—it is not about using tools for an appearance of convenience, but as spirit teaches. Anyone who needs to ask where the difference lies does not understand the ways Sasabonsam teaches.

Within the cape of Papa Bones there are many veins and many rooms and it is rarely experienced that the family of spirits belonging to Obeah have become adversaries in relation to already existing spirits in the house of the seeker, as this spirit host resonates with your very own skeleton. It thus follows that the prime technique of Obeah is what we have come to know as Shamanism. Shamanism in this context means a technology for entering into contact with the spirits of Nature—these being by seeking out places of power, the use of herbs or drinks—for the sake of being tutored by the legions of Sasabonsam and Papa Bones and being gifted their particular power as they resonate with the structure of the Obeahman.

Papa Bones can be seen as the magical multi-verse, the source of power and the ability to bewitch. There are as many different Lord Bones as there are bones in our body. Each and every one has specific attributes and specific vibrational qualities that can be brought into work as the foot of the Obeahman walks on the points of the particular obiya he was granted.

In addition to his or her skeleton being a composite of many spirits he carries within his cape the realm of animals and insects. Deities associated with the trafficking of spirits are found here, like the serpent, *Sarato*, the turtle, *Morocoi*, the spider, Anansi and a host of spirits from the greenwood. The moth is of special importance as the carrier of the hidden flame of obiya. A moth killing itself in the candles set out for Papa Bones is indeed a good omen. But beyond these, Papa Bones cannot work without his messenger. This messenger is found within the family of Anima Sola. Anima Sola is the saint associated with the spirits in purgatory. In the Roman Apostolic Church masses to her are called *Sufragetium*—masses of suffering. The mystery around her is great and we shall return to this mystery in full later on. For now it is important to impart that it is Anima Sola that seals the obiya by infecting the Obeahman/woman with a dread known as the 'trial of fire'. Until this occurs the Obeahman/woman is not truly an obiya. This affirmation can occur by nightmares of a fiery nature—always followed by waking up in a shamanic fever. It can also be a process. For instance one Obeahwoman reports that her trial of fire occurred by 'hot' dreams where she saw the hairy feet of Anima Sola and her following in fields of fern. The dream ignited bubbles of cold fire wandering around in her body for an extended period of time resulting in a physical explosion in her workspace. From this the fire was transplanted upon the skeleton and the obiya was seated.

Anima Sola is born from the Mother of the Lake. Not any lake, but the lake of pitch spoken of earlier. This lake is the mother of Anima Sola and the possession of pitch from this lake connects one naturally to the root of Obeah. There is a mysterious connection between Asase, the mother of the lake, and Papa Bones since neither of them relates to each other in spite of their contract of marriage, but Anima Sola is always used as their intermediary.

The reception of the power of Obeah, the initiation, is always given by an Obeahman in succession. It is a heritage and thus it can only be passed down from skeleton to skeleton. The ways of initiation can take many forms; the object is always about what is the most effective avenue of passing down the obiya. This can range from complex formats to a quite simple passing on of powers. The mystery at play is related to Anima Sola, as the one who seals and quickens the power given. Without her intervention and blessing the obiya given is simply a dormant power and no Obeahman is rising from flames not lightened. In the end, spirit makes an Obeahman; human intervention just opens the roads for the birth of the Obeahman/woman being a possibility. Some Obeahmen/women are also given spirit pots of Papa Bones and Anima Sola, but these are not a prerequisite as the obiya is after all something that will rest in the foundation of your body, the skeleton. All genuine Obeahmen/women do however hold some form of 'Obeahbox' which can be incorporated in the spirit vessels or be a spiritual object apart.

As we see, the gatherings of spirits involved in the practice of Obeah are not many. The multiplicity enters as Obeah is worked and spirit contact made. What we find is that Sasabonsam is the source for the sasa/obiya the Obeahman possesses. The obiya is given by mediation of Papa Bones and sealed and quickened by Anima Sola. So from this, Obeah is a power given and it is up to the Obeahman to develop, understand and make sense of the obiya. Obeah will never take the shape of a system or something neatly organized, because obeah is something personal—it is the root for creating one's own world lodged in the spirit connections made. Obeah is an enormous vault of intelligent powers you can communicate with mainly by using trance states and searching out places of power, but also by the use of dice and candles consecrated in special and secret ways. Obiya is about your soul set aflame in spiritual congruence and in this way the Obeahman is the maker of his or her own ontology made possible by manipulation of the transmutative matter inherited in the cosmic matrix. In this way the Obeahman is reminiscent of the modern Chaos magician but instead of sensitivity with social paradigms he or she holds sensitivity with the shifting arches of creation. This mystery is what Papa Bones teaches and can never be conferred in a 'passing on of power' that simply ignites this journey toward becoming obiya. The process of becoming is mediated by the newly seeded one as he or she understands the power seeking to lodge in his or her skeleton. It is a path of failure and triumph—it is a path of bad luck and fortune—where you become the smith of your own fortune and wisdom.

The root of Obeah as known in Trinidad has been a guarded secret for a long time, but I have decided, as Papa Bones allowed, to present the root of the power of Obeah in a way given to me by Papa Bones himself taking possession of my tutor. And so, here I present the transmission known as:

THE HYPOSTASIS OF
ABYSINA CLARISSA AND THE GREEN BEASTS

In the threshold-house there came
two men of a green complexion
Those were the guardians of the Mine of Old

Later that day when the Sun had sung its song
for the Sleep of the Ocean
The principles of Old came forth
from the Blood of the field of pitch

They laughed in silent screams and took away
the doll from its heart
In its place they installed a hook and
a gleaming Stone of Weird Scent

Calmly, they arrived to the Surface of the forgotten Kingdom
and they held Her in their bosom and violently and beastly
they stabbed their vivid essence inside of Her womb

Time passed by and Shame turned into
the revenge of Peace upon the Water-Earth

I came forth through forbidden gates—a child of mother and
beasts. I came riding along crooked paths—my eyes of moist
death and my skin of Angelic Beauty

My Mother, my Love—my father, my Beast-Love
and He who turned the axe
Into gold above my groin with ghostly declarations
She, my mother, a queen, my Beast-Love

with the wild Hair, her Love-nest
We all triads of Holy Intercourse and I
the un-begotten of Life

My Mother, the Sun—the green beasts of foreign Origin,
my father's of Death
And then the journey began. The black and violet one which
comes forth in the blood and rocks of memory and time

And violence is my name and nature as All and Nothing.
Words—too hurtful
Ivory-Earth and the lashes of Fire. Death to the Beast-Child.
Chains and molestations Chained in Death
and Love's distress

My mother's Scream and Her lover's laughter. The man-beast-
he was watching and took his joy in the act of the Eyes.

Screams in the night. My doll gone and my un-begotten birth
gave me differences

This text speaks about the patterns of formation that generate the spirit Anima Sola—but it also speaks of the Mother of the Pitch Lake and what type of forces Papa Bones made pacts and contracts with. So on one side, he mediates Sasabonsam, and on the other he is mediated by Anima Sola and the Mother of the Pitch Lake. There is also a secret interpretation of the text, but in the scope of this text the presentation of the text alone will suffice.

Besides herbal medicines and poisons, the activities of the Obeahman are largely confined to the trade of the exorcist and spirit-catcher in the form of duppies and shadows. Some words about the spirits we find in Caribbean legends will provide a better image of the spiritual landscape in question.

The first class of spirits is duppies, also known as *jumbies*. They are usually associated with ghosts and fairies but are also similar to the *lares* and *larvaes* of Roman households—and also vampires. A duppy in its most simplified understanding is an inhabitant of some invisible state, realm or ray whose actions in the mundane reality are tangible. We find in Trinidad the custom of throwing rice grains at the front and back of the house as a means for protection against duppies. Legend tells that the duppy must stop and count the grains before it walks on. In Europe this technique is found to be used mostly to ward off revenants and vampires. Likewise we find some accounts of the protective abilities of rosebushes as an aid in warding off duppies as they get tangled on the thorns when they stop to smell the roses. Salt is also a remedy that figures frequently in order to ward them off one's house, which in European legends is a remedy for keeping malevolent fairies at bay. Duppies are believed to be purely nocturnal, and cannot stand the light of day. As we see from the spiritual technology involved, a duppy is considered to be a harmful spirit; it can be a revenant, a vampire, vengeful spirits of nature in general or hostile fairies. These are the kind of spirits that the Obeahman is a specialist in tracking, trapping and expelling. As such he serves the function of exorcist or expeller. The greatest defense is however the 'duppy bead', a red and black seed that by itself serves as a guard against duppies and malefica.

We have then the class of spirits known as *douens*; Anima Sola is not only one of them, but also their guide and Queen. From the text quoted earlier we can learn what the inner dimensions of this mystery is about. They are known to approach residents at night, sulking and crying to tempt people to chase them—just to get them lost in the woods. The bewilderment of tracking is made even more disturbing by their backward-turned feet. Popular folklore tells they are the souls of un-baptized children, but the mystery goes deeper than this and has little to do with baptism or its lack. These spirits are messengers between the worlds. Their presence represents the thin veil that separates the invisible from the visible, death from life; in this they are a dangerous force—spirits directly connected to Sasabonsam. Sasabonsam is represented by the Odum/Ceiba/Silk Cotton tree. He is a refuge for the duppies and douens. When spirits go out in the world we can see them as lights moving around trees and they can also manifest like St. Elmo's fire and wandering lightning. In Trinidad and Tobago the lights are known as *Jacakalantan*—obviously a corruption of 'Jack o' Lantern'. These lights are reputed to guide the curious into No-Man's Lands, other realms, and to guide people's disappearances in nature.

Lugarhoo or the werewolf is another spirit related to Obeah. The Lugarhoo, probably itself a corruption of the French *loup-garou*, is said to hold an obiya made from carefully selected roots and sticks that enables its transformation. It is considered to be an avatar of Sasabonsam speaking of the transformative quality of the Silk Cotton tree, whose nature is that of a wolf, both in caring for its pack and its stalking and hunting disposition. It should be said that some Obeahmen insist on this transformation being purely physical and often this is a transformation that occurs from the waist down. This transformation is made possible by possessing a particular obiya.

Spirits in league with the Obeahman are spirits like the *Soucouyant* who is also known as *La Diablesse*, and whose most famous avatar is probably *Gang Gang Sara*. Gang Gang Sara is said to have been taken by the wind from Africa and brought to the village of Les Coteaux where she gained her living as a wise woman. La Diablesse on the other hand, with her eyes of burning coal and corpse-like skin, is in a very different vibration. With La Diablesse we find the theme of abduction in the woods, but also seduction and madness. She is a type of vampire, a lamia that stalks men and seeks their death. She can show herself as a true mademoiselle with a preference for baroque clothing. While the La Diablesse is similar to the vampire, the Soucouyant is more akin to shape-shifters.

Mama Dlo should also be mentioned. She is believed to be one of the lovers of Papa Bois, and is the only force in nature Sasabonsam respects and is able to humble himself in front of. She is a mermaid—but not only this, as with her anaconda body and human torso she is the Queen of mermaids. The respect earned by Sasabonsam is replicated in her vengeance upon people that abuse the woods and nature. Those who show no respect for what sustains them—namely nature in all her red glory—will at times be visited by Mama Dlo. She can come in the form of a seductive young woman, or as a natural catastrophe with a surprisingly limited area of destruction, namely the wrongdoer's house and haven. We find stories in local folklore of how Papa Bois calls upon her aid when people misbehave in Nature and she brings a host of mysterious devastations onto the people involved. She is also known to be able to walk on land and if she does so she will gravitate to the woods, to Papa Bois and Sasabonsam where she hunts and punishes together with them and their spirit herd. Mama Dlo is the Queen of the many mermen and mermaids. Their father is said to be Leviathan. People who had their shadow caught or sasa removed can go to the mermen and mermaids and ask for its restoration. But this comes with a price—and often a pact, and the pact usually ends in death or *tristesse*. However when a pact is made and it is desired to end it, it is said that one should bring a pair of one's best shoes to the ocean shore and here state that this is payment for the services, these shoes and nothing but these shoes. You will then burn one shoe and throw the other one into the ocean.

All these spirits heed one particular offering, which is calabash and maize bread. I have found a good way to prepare this is to make dough of cornbread using yellow maize and fill a pumpkin-shell with it. This pumpkin-baked bread is then brought to the ocean shore or to the Silk Cotton tree—or any other tree where you have witnessed the Jacakalantan being active. This offering is given tobacco, rum and olive oil, and the spirit of the place is called. The Obeahman always knows that this is done by connecting heart with heart—and from this the enchantment is sung and spun.

Chapter III

The Kabalistic Banquette of Lemegeton

When I was introduced to Obeah I was also introduced to the '*Kabalistic banquette*'. The banquette is similar to the banquette we find set for Bawon Samedi and the Ghuede on All-Hallows or the commemoration of the Mighty Dead found in some strains of Traditional Craft. The table is covered with a black tablecloth and fine china is placed, along with nice silverware. On the table is presented red wine, rum, water, and bread and in some instances red meat, spiced and lightly fried or baked. Under each plate sigils are drawn and also under the corresponding chair. Candles, white or black, are lit under the chair. A master of the ceremonies is appointed and given a lash and a sword. On the table is also present a copy of Waite's '*The Book of Black Magic*', Lemegeton, *The Grimoire of Honorius* or *Grimorium Verum*—although Waite's book, like de Laurence's *The Great Book of Magical Art*, are the most frequent magical books present at the banquette table. The participants are murmuring the names of their daimonic attendants as they partake of the foods, and possession occurs in a direct manner. The Master of Ceremonies will with lash restrain unruly spirits, and with sword challenge them to show good conduct.

Obviously the banquette has borrowed from Freemasonry, but the context is very different as here demons are invited to descend, give counsel or perform feats of magic—all under the supervision of Papa Bones, also known as the Prince of Evil.

De Laurence's *Great Book* is basically a manual of Christian Theosophy leaning heavily on what he refers to as 'Hindoo magic', hence one of the many epitaphs given to Obeahmen in the 19th Century was 'Hindoo doctor'. There is however a great amount of spiritual technology referred to in this work that Obeahmen used as they saw fit, and given that de Laurence borrowed heavily from Waite, Hartman and Levi we can see a congruence of influences enforcing the importance of Waite's encyclopedic *Book of Black Magic*.

De Laurence wrote extensively about the ways of summoning spirits. He suggests 'hindoo' models where one is seated in a circle and calls the spirit in the fumes— also found in the works of Levi. There are also formats of banquette of a Kabalistic nature inspired by the design of the temple of Solomon, which in turn calls upon some Masonic influence.

In Trinidad the main book in the cult of Obeah is Waite's *Book of Ceremonial Magic* together with the psalms. Goetic evocations are read aloud at the banquettes, those who attend are dressed nicely and will participate in the banquette with aristocratic manners, though if any act out of line they will be brought back to place by the warden. Both demons and animalistic spirits are able to possess people at these banquets. When these Kabalistic spirits appear in ceremonies and services for other spirits it is customary to chase them away so that the ritual purity can be held intact.

There are many ways of performing the kabalistic banquette. Some are reminiscent of the *Misa Espiritual* and others follow a more ceremonial format. One format

is clearly adapted from the writings of Eliphas Levi and de
Laurence's *The Great Book of Magical Art* as in the following
illustration:

AN INVOCATION BY BURNING TEMPLE INCENSE.

The kabbalistic shrine is decorated with the hexagram
and food and drink for the spirit is placed upon it, flanked
by white, yellow, black, and red candles while incense is
burned. The incense is a particular blend of herbs, seeds
and resins that may or may not be blended with common
Church incense.

The procedure most used is the format of a table
banquette. The procedure is fairly simple and invites
a creative use of seals and summoning adapted for the
purpose from the Solomonic tradition. The Obeahman
will on the table mark with chalk—or cornmeal—a
crossroad. At each end he will mark a circle where the
proper seals are inscribed. At each seat a circle will also be
inscribed with a line stretching from this circle to the main
cross marked on the table. Around each chair a triangle
is marked with its upper point towards the centre of the
table, which can be with or without Solomonic names.

At the four circles in the cross the seal of Papa Bones is marked in the South, Morocoi in the West, Sarato in the North and Anansi in the East. The seal of the intelligence, demon, spirit or angel that one seeks to call upon is marked in the separate circles and also in the triangle under the chair. Alternatively magical squares can be used. A Master of ceremonies is appointed and also a warden. The warden is given a whip and a sword/cane and the master holds solely his Obeah-cane. On the table is water, alcoholic beverages, bread and red raw meat. Incense is burned at the south where the master sits, and here a generous portion of apricot brandy is placed.

Prior to the main summoning everyone needs to purify the soles of their feet, palms, throat and top of the head with a mixture of cassia and olive oil.

The Master of Ceremonies will then conduct the summoning of the spirits and those participants assigned the place of particular spirits will summon these spirits as the general summoning is made. This will lead to trance and possession of the spirits that then are fed through their devotee. As the ceremony proceeds and possession occurs the warden is assigned the task of maintaining order and control of the spirits; this can include whipping the mediums and also the destruction of seals and triangles by water and lashes to break any malevolent and dangerous possession. Needless to say, these banquets can be dramatic affairs.

Preliminary invocation:

"In the name of the most Holy and Sovereign Lord of Evil, he Master of the Houses and the spark from the

Dark, say Hail! To the Prince of the Dark as I ... in
the name of the black guardians of the secret lake of
pitch conjure thee to rise from within the broken egg
and give birth to more than a mere phantom-image in
this infernal square where the spheres of Heaven and
Hell are conjured."

The master will then chant or sing forth the name of the
entity that he wants to appear, using whatever mediumistic
techniques desired.

Conjuring:

"Listen *as I give sound to the words of power. Secret*
words and commands that bind and restrict ye to enter
this world and feast with no intent of harm amongst
these servants of the most Dark Lord, the Prince Himself,
because it is by him I summon and command you.

RESINUS KARAPAMEK ZEBULON RETAS

"With these words the Spell of Binding is set in motion
and the wheels of Hell are closing in under the fire of
the Stars.

"Give your tongue to these vessels, old spirits, and rise
up in all your youth to return into the flesh of Beauty.
This is the zone of transmission where the mirror cracks
and the spirits are set free in all its limitation.

"Your care and willingness is your Sword and you
spirits of the Dark should heed the Sword of Satan

well since this token is given unto me, in my office on Earth; by the Prince of Hell this right has been given to me. As the whip and this rite is given for the sake of conjuration of you with these tools of obiya. In the name of the Prince of Darkness, The Lord of Hell, Satan Apepe, Bones of the Death and Bones of the Cross whose name is Legion I command you (name the spirit) to obey my authority and give me correct and fruitful answers in this banquette made to your honor."

The banquette is then ended with a farewell to the spirits executed by the master of Ceremonies and the Warden in tandem whereupon salt water is poured over the heads of the participants as the ceremony is at an end.

This format can also be used for scrying and be reduced to the participation of as few as two people. The basic format is followed, but instead of allowing the spirit to take possession of flesh, a triangle of art with the seal is marked at the centre of the table with the four lines making up the crossroad running from the triangle to the four corners. Offerings are then placed on the seal and a mirror, crystal ball and heavy incense is presented on the seal while the spirit is called by name alone.

There is also an oracle by using dice that can be utilized. These dice are consecrated in a particular way and are interpreted in conformity with Kabbalah, more precisely, the Sephiroth. Two dice are needed, which are interpreted as follows as they fall in Malkuth:

2	Yesod	7	Chesed
3	Netzasch	8	Binah
4	Hod	9	Chockmah
5	Tipareth	10	Kether
6	Geburah	11 & 12	go outside the tree and thus the dice are unresponsive.

Even numbers are interpreted as negative and odd numbers as positive—but the quality is mediated by the sephirotic temperament, although they can be used for simple yes and no answers.

The Obeahman will use the dice by placing them in a glass of apricot brandy and saying:

Papa bones, by your intercessor Abysina Clarissa, give me true answer.

He will then drink the dice, meaning, he drinks the brandy but leaves the dice in his mouth while reciting:

Gwangwela Gedehusu

The Obeahman will recite these spirit names until the 'doubt' appears clear in his mind. He will then spit out the dice. For additional questions he will rub his hands in apricot brandy and throw the dice from both hands, meaning one dice in each hand. Of importance here is the state of mind when the dice are tossed. He needs to be in a calm and receptive state; better if the state calls upon dream—because through the oracle he will ascend and descend on the ladders of meaning.

SEAL OF ANANSI

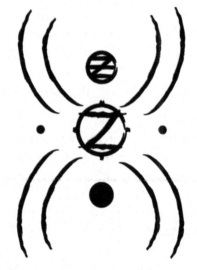

SEAL OF SARATO

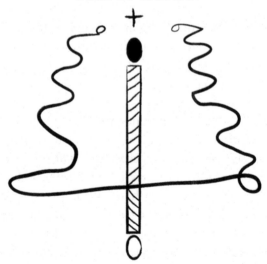

Chapter IV

The Abyss of the Lone Fire

A Prayer to Our Lady of Solitude

As the slain Deer I offer myself
To the flames on the tomb of infinity
I bid thee Mother of Solitude to come in
I am all Soliloquy and serenity

One step I take within the flames
I am the torch of Solitude
And I am the One of many Names
I am the Iron of Your Chains
And I am the One, ever-chained

Lustrous and severe I gaze
Upon and within
I am the All consuming contraction
The Naught and the Sin

See me as I fold my hands
And raise them to the skies
See me as I burn in silent sorrow
And smother my blood with
Your silent prayer

You are my harbor and my Hell
My priestess and deepest sadness
One step I take and enter within
Enter the embrace of all souls' solitude
As the very breath of my flesh!

ANIMA SOLA IS THE LEADER OF THE DOUEN AND THE messenger-daughter of Papa Bones. But as we have seen earlier, she is not really the daughter of Papa Bones, but the result of assault and aggression. She is the spirit of solitude as she leads the many douen. She is a child of the Moon; hence her gift is that of '*kumona*', meaning 'to see'. Kumona implies both foresight and spirit sight. The douen mystery is profound and holds a relationship with the *Mysté Marassa* in Vodou—but also the Yoruba *Abiku* phenomena (infant death syndrome). What these mysteries have in common with Anima Sola is the way they speak about the thin veil between the worlds, how we are always walking in the company of death and spirits. It is simply a question of being able to 'see' them.

Douen is derived from the Latin *duende*, synonymous with goblins and brownies Northern Europe, whilst in Iberia and South America the category also encompasses fairies and any green short-grown spirit.

If we add to this the Catholic imagery of the lonely soul in Hell who chooses to stay in hellfire with the chains broken we find the explanation for this iconic representation in the story telling about her hypostasis. It is also in the Catholic apocrypha we find an explanation for her association with the Prince of Darkness. One story tells of a certain Anima Sola, called *Celestina Abednago*. Her last name is a reference to one of the prophets the Babylonian king Nebuchadnezzar throws into the fires in the Book of Daniel—but the fire does not hurt him. Celestina was said to go to Calvary on Good Friday with wine and water to the crucified ones. Arriving at Calvary she gave wine and water to Dismas and Gestas who were crucified alongside with Jesus, but not to Jesus for whom she held contempt. In response to her refusal to give him wine and water he cursed her to suffer thirst in the fires of purgatory.

We also find the icon of Anima Sola in Palo Mayombe where she is known, amongst many names, as *Mayanet Viento Malo*—a bitter hot wind of destruction. Anima Sola is also used to depict the Vodou mysté *Marinette Pie Cheche* and *Marinette Ge Rouge*. Marinette is considered one of the more dangerous of the Lwa and is intimately connected to the woods, the domain of Papa Bois/Gran Bwa as is the nkisi Mayanet.

From this we see a theme taking shape; Anima Sola is the Moon's dead daughter that serves as a messenger between worlds. She is a spirit of torment, a hot bitter wind that can literally drag you to Hell. Hell must be understood as a metaphor for otherness, and the woods are where we find these gates and portals to otherness. Hence she is the messenger for the Lord of Darkness, the fire that casts a white shadow in the night and transforms in agonizing ways. Hence she is also the patron for the mystery of loup garou/werewolves. Sympathy with Santisima Muerte can also be seen.

We can work with this tormented spirit, this messenger between worlds, by paying attention to the stations of the moon. Her offerings are water, fruit juices, mints and chocolates. She is never given alcohol as this is said to agitate her negatively. The classical icon of Anima Sola serves well as a point of entrance and it is this form that will be envisioned when the Obeahman works with the stations of the moon. It is this form he will see taking on nuances in accord with the ways the moon walks through the zodiac. Some guidelines for such contemplative work with the spirit of solitude are as follows—these lunar stations can be seen as the spirit herd of Anima Sola, while she herself finds her own station in the new and full moon.

When the moon is new see her in a full-body egg-shaped halo flickering in deep blue with rays of white lightning. Her face is veiled in black.

When the moon is full see her burning in a white circumference with green vipers stretching up from her feet and joining in the flames encompassing her completely as fire takes over the moon.

When the moon enters Aries see her with the dove of the Holy Spirit descending upon her. In this station we can ask to remove sorrow—or we can ask that sorrow is given.

When the moon enters Taurus see her with multiple blue eyes and we can petition for the gift of kumona.

When the moon enters Gemini her hellfire takes on a purple shade and she wears a crown of pearls. In this station she inspires the mind and tongue and gives eloquence as much as confusion.

When the moon enters Cancer the Obeahman finds a station good for contemplation and her form is marine, her hands covered with scales and the hellfire turns blue and liquid. It is here we can find the joy of solitude, and it is also a station useful for receiving the gift of visions.

When the moon is in Leo she takes the form of a dry and wooden girl with closed eyes, who appears to be consumed with delight in hellfire.

When the moon turns into Virgo she is prone to cause the Obeahman to remember her sorrow and stories. She is surrounded by fields of rye and wheat in flames. Dreams can be particularly vivid in this station.

When the moon is in Libra she is red from blood and is constantly bleeding in stigmata. Around her is a field of roses—in flames. This station can be beneficial for creative solitude.

When the moon enters Scorpio she takes the form of a young girl, like in her classical icon. It is in this station she assumes the name Abysina Clarissa and presides over seduction, sexuality and violence.

When the moon is in Sagittarius she is standing on the seed known as Solomon's Seal and stretches tall as her hands join with the Hellfire in her accumulation of magical heat and fire. It is a station good to work for the sake of fashioning or consecrating talismans and magical objects.

When the moon is in Capricorn she shows herself in black veils, but her face is uncovered, and her black eyes stare right at you in a commanding manner. The hellfire is a field of yellow roses. This station is good for work of authority and dominion. Life might be taken in this station.

When she moves into Aquarius she is robed with the starry skies and fires are burning from wounds in her hands and feet, she cries fire and roses as she lifts one hand in a posture of benediction. This station is one of healing and painful comfort.

When the moon enters Pisces she is seen as a young girl in fires hovering over a black ocean who feeds herself on her own tears. This station represents the comfort of loneliness and the dread of being.

The stations of this sorrowful mystery can be seen both as fields of teaching and contact—but also fields of activity, where conjoined with the waxing and waning of the moon spellcraft and contact work can be undertaken. The technique used is to give her offerings and then lie down and enter trance. This work is 'shamanic' in essence.

The Obeahman will present to her leaves of peppermint, a strong red juice containing no alcohol, light one single red candle and call forth a sensation of intense solitude, taste the curse of all your cares and due to your observation of the moon allow the sorrowful virgin of power to come forth as your boat and bring you to the domains of the lone spirit. The Obeahman will ask to be flogged naked in front of the messenger as he asks her to open the vaults of clarity. She is the pyre upon which all impurities and all wrongdoings are dissolved into smoke. In the smoke the letters will be written and the letters will aid the Obeahman in the path.

The Obeahman can also enter directly into the lunar sphere that is ruling the night and, well-attuned to the lunar vibration, he will visualize a heat building up from your toes. When it hits the groin he will notice an even bigger pyre that is licking his body from somewhere below. He will allow himself to be consumed by the flames. Totally consumed in flames, he will notice that heavy chains are painfully attached to his wrists. In this state he will whisper his screams, ask her to come before him and give him something, to drink from her abodes of honey-juice and mint. He will ask her to sweeten his life as he seeks to understand her mystery—and pray intensely from the heart in a spirit of helpless spontaneity.

The Obeahman can also, through acts of summoning, become Her with every cell of flesh and every drop of blood. In such a risky undertaking he needs to strive towards creating a state of intense suffering and find release in this suffering. This is a way of forcing 'the trial of fire' to occur where she will be the Obeahman's teacher and guide. Another way of bringing her is to make a rosary in sequences of nine and formulate a simple oration where one asks Abysina Clarissa, Anima Sola to unfold in the land of the Obeahman's dreams. The Obeahbox or the Obeahvessels should then be placed under the bed and a yellow and a red candle be lit. The red candle should be placed at the level of the head and the yellow at the level of the feet.

In her school, Sorrow is the Master and Teacher and the sorcerer appeasing her should be centered enough to understand the complexity of the pain evoked when the worship of the lone soul in tormenting fire is approaching you. Meditation on her imagery should be done frequently in order for her to come in haste to the sorcerer's call.

There is also one other method for facilitating contact with her that follows the format of a mass. This might appear sacrilegious in the scope of her history and rejection of Christ—and indeed it is. In this way the Obeahman uses heresy to provide absolution...

A Kabalistic Mass for Anima Sola Mayanet
For the cultivation of Kumona, the ability to "see".

The Obeahman will prepare the altar with the icon of Anima Sola. Her icon can be the Catholic icon or a female doll dressed in black and red. In front of it he will light one red candle and one black candle. The Obeahman will kneel in front of her with eyes closed and recount her history as a child of rape and death at a too young age. He will enter the mourning point of sorrow as breath leaves her body and the blood quits in her veins. He will identify with this point where carnal life leaves and the divine afflatus enters, allowing his breath to follow this pattern (using only his nose, with his mouth closed). He will do this until his body has entered a state of total relaxation and calamity in the centre of the sorrowful distress of Anima Sola's birth, rise to your feet and call forth the four evangelists:

We call upon the Apostle of Transmission of the East, Matthew
We call upon the Apostle of Transmission of the South, Mark
We call upon the Apostle of Transmission of the West, Luke
We call upon the Apostle of Transmission of the North, John.

Conclude with reading from Ezekiel 1:4-14

The Obeahman will spend a short time in meditation and be aware how the winds of the quarters are blowing into his temple.

READING:

Ezekiel 7: 5-11 and Song of Solomon chapter 4. These two readings being the carrier of the essence of praise of Anima Sola, the ritually butchered girl-child of Old, She who was ripped open by the Old Ones from the Stars.

LECTION:

As the rage of the Fathers has entered down upon the Earth so will the beauty of the Daughters be a blessing unto the priest. Just as electrical dark and the child, the thunder and storm, will give rise to mornings fair and blue, so shall the anger be planted amongst the brethren and the beauty be born thereof. Such are the ways of Mayanet, the slaughtered girl child, daughter of the Holy Bones that at all times and again and again will rise in the cemetery of the Thunderstorm and make fair and perfect the air blowing from all corners of the earth. She is the fairest and the youngest of all the objects of the spirit of desire. The curse has been born and the blessing is born there from. Therefore ye shall all remember that in the painstaking fire of the curse the blessing is its child. Therefore ye shall remember that restrained and bound the child of captivity is freedom. Just as Lord Lucifer the Great used his Cell of Condemnation as his Temple of Black Contemplation, so shall you also partake in the contemplation of night in the hour where pottery is crashed—and the life of the believer made into terror. Remember the power of the Lord. And ye shall remember how he turned his condemnation into eternal Oblivion and then into a ladder of rejoice into the Heavens of Honeydew. The Lord of the Holy Bones is the King of Zombee and the spirit giving it life and Light. Through the powers of the Lord and the twin girls of the Holy Mass, the black and the white are set into play and a multitude of pathways are open as dozens of rainbows pour forth from the infernal kingdom and out into the blessing peace of the freed slaves.

The Obeahman will now kneel down in front of her, this time with eyes open, and look upon her image with affection and rejoice in her wonders. He will now call her forth and perform the Holy Eucharist of Anima Sola, the spirit of the dead girl child who is also known as Mayanet and Abysina Clarissa.

THE LITANY:

Strong daughter of the Fire	*Come down upon us*
Guide of the hidden portals	*Come down upon us*
Bestower of joy and relief	*Come down upon us*
Daughter of perfection	*Come down upon us*
Daughter of many sorrows	*Come down upon us*
Daughter of infernal fire	*Come down upon us*
Daughter who broke the chains	*Come down upon us*
Daughter who broke the spell	*Come down upon us*
Daughter who masters the craft	*Come down upon us*
Daughter who guards the Obeah	*Come down upon us*
Daughter who is the One	*Come down upon us*
Daughter who is the many	*Come down upon us*
Daughter who is Naught	*Come down upon us*

Anima Sola, daughter of the Sacred Bones	*Blessed be*
Anima Sola daughter of the Lady of the Lake	*Blessed be*
Anima Sola the pitch-dark messenger of Light	*Blessed be*
Anima Sola who is Mayanet, who is Abysina Clarissa	*Blessed be*

We pray that you come down upon this your body (chocolate or mint) *and the chalice filled with your dark blood* (juice of red fruits—no alcohol).

The Obeahman will extend his arms over the Eucharist and say the following:

SASA-SAMANA-SASA-SAMANA
May the Lord Bones bless these sacraments
SASA-SAMANA-SASA-SAMANA
May the Mother of the Pitch Lake bless these sacraments
SASA-SAMANA-SASA-SAMANA
May Anima Sola, daughter of the lake come down upon this body and blood and make it alive for the sake of Kumona. Let me see with your eyes into the mysteries of being and unbeing. May this power rest within me now and forever more SASA-SAMANA Blessed be Abysina Clarissa!

When consuming the sacraments the Obeahman will visualize that a fire from the abdomen sprouts forth and attacks his eyes from the inside with great force. This might lead to possession, clairvoyance and a state of oracular frenzy.

CHAPTER V

ANANSI'S TRAIL IN SASABONSAM'S WORLD

FOR THE WISI, PAPA BONES AND ALL OF THE SPIRITS THE Obeahman works with are known as *kromanti*. Kromanti means 'flying ones'; they are connected with air, and the obeah spirits with hot air. Kromanti can mingle with spirits of other elements, like Papa Bones is hot air mingling with earth. One Wisiman I met (who saw Obeah as a form of Bokor-craft) told me that he saw Papa Bones as a horned skeletal figure resting within a tornado with blazing suns for eyes. This imagery brings into light his elemental composition of wind, earth, fire and dominion. In the Winti faith we find a similar cosmology as in Obeah. For the Winti, Anansi reflects the essence of *Anana* (God). The godhood is a network of connections, not unlike the 231 gates in Luria's Kabbalah, and I believe it is such similarities that led to Obeah being seen as a practical Kabbalah that influenced Obeahmen to resort to such usage of 'Kabbalah' in its original sense of being a prophetic reception of divine mysteries. The Winti also have a female form of Papa Bones known as *Mama Aisa*—perhaps borrowed from the Vodoun Aizan through her totem, the yellow python. She is a caring and benevolent spirit, but she can also take the form of *Sofia Bada,* who induces bleeding from the genitals and eyes when she takes possession of the Obeahman/woman. When she takes this form she call upon dogs and wolves and with this comes Anima Sola. There are also kromantis known as *Indyi*, which are the spirits of indigenous priests and shamans that continued to influence the world upon death as teacher spirits.

Papa Bones is, amongst some Winti and Wisi, also called King Seven and seven are the kromantis that are under his direct ministry. As King Seven he is also known as *Yaw*, which signifies 'Fire from Heaven'. Papa Bones is also associated with St. Ezekiel, St. Gabriel, St. Expeditus and even Sta. Lucia. Some Sango Baptists see him as King Esu, but largely his feast day is said to be the 19th of April, the feast day of St. Expeditus.

Other kromantis are *Opete*, the Vulture that easily possesses the Obeahman, particularly those Obeahmen that are ruled by flying totemic forces. *Adyaini*, the jaguar, is another important kromanti. Then we have restless warrior spirits like *Adumakuku*, *Bonwaku*, *Tando*, *Ananka* and *Aladi* , which are kromantis often used by the Obeahman. These kromantis are all Indyi, and are intimately lodged within the mysteries of Sasabonsam.

In addition we have spirits of the bush, like *Apuku* and the spirit of the termite-hill, *Akantasi*. These are wintis, or elemental spirits that can be used together with the kromanti to work Wisi or obiya. There is also the spirit known as *Luwangu*, the spirit of muddy waters, that is very demanding and claims submission and great respect when called forth. Lastly we have the mischievous dwarf spirit called *Bakru*, who is a servant of Sasabonsam and loves trickery, alcohol and jewels.

We have also other spirits of a shamanic nature like *Morocoi*, the tortoise, *Sarato*, the snake, *Mothra*, the Moth and *Anansi*, the Spider, to mention a few. The signatures of these spirits are often very simple and figurative. After all, the craft of the Obeahman is a mystery. Everything is developed as a consequence of true rapport with the spirits of obeah and the possession of obiya. In this sense the craft of each Obeahman is a secret art that is developed between the Obeahman and spirit. Trance states, possession, 'shamanic journeys' and automatic writings were the tools I was introduced to—but for another Obeahman the tools of ingress might be different. The obiya will always forge a path unique inasmuch as it will resist any system or order that makes sense for many. Obeah is and will be a sorcerous path for the empowered individual.

A simpler way for the Obeahman to work with these spirits consists of erecting a simple altar where he will have present a glass of apricot brandy, and yellow, red, black and white candles. The altar will be placed in the centre of his working area. Under the altar he will draw a seal of a simple circle with a cross in the middle. The cross should enter through the circle on all four edges. He will then draw another circle around the altar. He might use cornflour, cascarilla, pemba, chalk or whatever he uses to mark spirit-signs. He should have a large piece of paper ready, and can perform the ritual in one of two ways. In both ways alcohol (rum, gin, vodka) and cigar or pipe are necessary. Either with internal recitation of the chosen deity's name, or recitation in a monotone whisper, he draw signs that occur to him in pure automata. Another procedure is as follows:

The Obeahman will smoke large amounts of cigar and sprinkle the area of the working with strong alcohol, drinking some yourself as well. He will start talking to the spirit in his mother-tongue or any other language that feels natural for him to speak in. He will blow cigar-smoke to

the corners of the altar and the working area and shout for
the spirit. He will use whatever he knows works to induce
trance-state or possession. Then he allows the spirit to do
what it wants with the paper. The kromanti spirit signs can
be used for further workings in the manner of serving as
a receiver for the forces called; they can be used as charms
and for healing purposes. The sacred dice are also an oracle
he can use, ruled by the spirits known as *Gwangwela* and
Gedehusu, the hands of Papa Bones, and are called upon to
give true answers as described in the third chapter.

The spirits of Obeah are infinite. Papa Bones is said to
consist of as many spirits himself as there are bones in the
body. He is a dynamic and deep vault of magical possibility.
The spirits that attach to the Obeahman are discovered
by a magical trance quite similar to the shamanic vision
quest. There are some components of importance here.
First of all, the Obeahman needs to sit or lie down at a tree
of 'bad repute', a tree known for its capacity for cursing.
Alternatively the Silk Cotton tree can be used. A fire is
made and resinous incense burned, with a preference for
benzoin and storax. Apricot brandy, rum and water are
poured at the root of the tree as he asks the spirit of the
tree, in the name of Papa Bones, to guide the journey.
The Obeahman will then see himself embraced by the
branches of the tree that takes him underground. Here he
needs to search for his spirit guide and ask the spirit guide
to take him to Anima Sola. When she is encountered the
Obeahman will ask her to take him to Papa Bones, who
will return the Obeahman to the land of the living.

As mentioned earlier, the sorcerous technology of
the Obeahman is largely related to duppy and shadow
catching. The Obeahman is able to catch these malevolent

spirits because these are spirits that gravitate towards him through his pact made with Papa Bones and Anima Sola. It is in this we find the association Obeah holds with 'bad fortune' and with the darker side of existence. Obeah bottles are also an integral part of the trade and are surprisingly similar to the European witch bottles where nails, metals, herbs and urine are the main components for making bottles of protection, and metals, herbs and rum for the purpose of catching duppies.

Some simple procedures for contact work consist of using words recited in a rhythmic fashion while the Obeahman uses the spirit seal as a gate for trance, and through this the sorcerous journey can begin.

A CALL TO PAPA BONES

The Obeahman will present two yellow candles at the centre of the altar, flanked by one red at the left and one black at the right. He will pour apricot brandy into a large jug and present it in front of himself, and then light a dark aromatic cigar and burn frankincense. He will use the following key to summon Papa Bones and will use these keys to open the door for trance.

> *Caché cache aamo*
> *Father of Bones*
> *Magid of Bones*
> *Concaru of bones*
> *Frenpé of Bones*
> *Shivering in thousands of suns*
> *Darkness caught*
> *At the summit of the third sun*

Pass on—in between
The scent of death
Blowing in the woods
Close the moon
Bring shadow to the sun
Bite through
Kakakaka hete!

A Call to Spirit Guides:

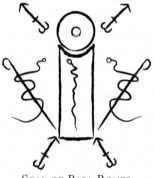

SEAL OF PAPA BONES

This call is used to summon duppies and spirit guides. For the Obeahman there is not much difference between Sasabonsam and Papa Bones' armies and the duppies in how they can be helpful for the Obeahman. He will present a glass of water and another one with spiced rum and light black and white candles smeared with the oil of orange flowers or honeysuckle. The Obeahman can also burn these scents in whatever way he finds proper. He will call repeatedly the following key, and as he senses the duppies arriving, will allow them to fill him as he sees himself turn into the form of Papa Bones:

Grave Cold spirits of Death
Ghosts that roam the night
Ghosts that roam my soul
I call you into my Shrine
The sore death
A fiery bleeding
In the smoke of Love
Grave Cold spirits of Death
Rest within my universe

A CALL TO ANIMA SOLA ABYSINA CLARISSA:

SEAL OF ANIMA SOLA ABYSINA CLARISSA

The Obeahman will prepare the altar with a cup of sweet fruit juice and light red candles in even numbers, making sure that everything is dark in his room or that night has fallen if this is done in the woods. He will draw her spirit sign and whisper her key:

Abysina, Abysina
The darkness is a hook
The darkness is a catcher
Coming after you
Is in you
Clarissa, Clarissa
Die in the name of the Moon

The Obeahman will meditate on her seal and bring her forth through the design as he engages his left hand in automatic drawing. While doing this he will recite:

The flaming night bearer
Of death
Molester and terminator
Molested and terminated
The silent dream
On the wings of hellfire
Queen of Suffering
I call upon you as my guide

He will light incense of myrrh to her praise and ask her to let him through as he opens up to her.

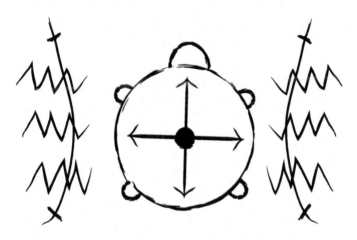

Morocoi, the turtle, is considered to be the prophetic power of Papa Bones. It is Morocoi that was one of the first creatures created, and who was the first animal to make a pact with Papa Bones. Morocoi represents endurance, the power of the silent hunter and wisdom of the ages. He can give foresight and prophecy and is called upon with offerings of white and blue candles, and rum steeped with cloves, cinnamon and star anise. The Obeahman will do this calling in a room totally dark, evoking space and the deep ocean into his being. This being done, he will light the candles and drink from the offering while reciting:

This is the testament of Morocoi's spell
In secret slumbering silence
Where the quarrels of emptiness rise
Look into dusty waters
And see the reflection of the past
Gleaming through
In elegancy

By the words of water and dust combined
Into the mortar and the pestle
You will conceive the truth
Of hardness
Dwelling in softness
The spell itself is a broken
Testimony between mothers
Sing the words of waves
And wind flashing into the mysterious
Darkness of the deep waters
Where sharks are allies
KOA AAH KOYOI AH MOROCOI

I will also present two rituals that can be performed by the consecrated Obeahman that follow a more ceremonial procedure. Naturally the elements of the rituals can—and should—for the Obeahman who has received the fire of kumona, be torn apart and used as need and will dictate. These are some examples of how to work the obiya and fortify it within the Obeahman.

MISSALE EZEKIEL SASABONSAM

Or the conjuration of the sorcerous Shadow-Self, A Black Mass for the constitution of the Obeahman and for the gaining of the power to charge fetishes and to command the spirits of the undead (zombee) and duppies.

PREPARATIONS:

The altar should be dressed in yellow and black. A rock should be presented, a gross, unpolished piece of stone. The master of the ritual will be armed with his cane and on the altar there should be present the Obeahbox. In this mass it is quite likely that further directions on the work will be given and adapted accordingly. Candles should be in the colours yellow (left) and black (right), with a small white candle in the middle between them. The Obeahman will stretch out his arms over the candles and make them powerful, declaring the following: "*I am ...., an Obeahman/woman in the House of Obeah and by the powers given to me from the Infernal Empire I hereby declare these candles to be infused with the power of the Prince of Darkness!*" He will then take some saliva and smear the candles with it. He will also have a glass and, if he prefers, some kind of representation of the flesh. He will use apricot brandy or a sweet, fruity white wine. He will be seated or standing, depending on his preference. He will light the candles and pour the glass full of wine. After the opening words have been said, he will also pour wine upon the rock presented. The rock will not be consecrated, but has an alchemical function in the ritual. His transformation will be mirrored in the features of the rock.

OPENING:

OKOMFO OBAJIFO OKOMFO OBAJIFO, *by the powers and auspices of the most high god upon the throne of the nine worlds.* NYANKONPON NYANKONPON OKOMFO OBAJIFO OKOMFO OBAJIFO NYANKONPON ODUM!

FIRST CONJURATION:

I have prostrated by flesh, blood and Bones in the centre of the world. I am the chalice! I am the blade! I am the burning saliva of the hot undead! I give unto the empires of the Shadow-makers my hands, feet, mouth and eyes. Let me receive the gift of the new eyes. KUMONA AYEEJE KUMONA AYEEJE KUMONA AYEEJE KUMONA. *I have entered into, beyond and further to the source of seeing! I am the source! I am the scourge! Within me rests the power of the snake. Within me rests the power of sasa. Within me rests the powers of saman. Burning self of the nine familiar ghosts, allow me to become the gate of death, the bridge towards my own ghostly being. Hot sasa, release from the hidden heart the powers of Obeah from the murky corners of the shadowy self and release the powers of air from the four corners of the world as the compass swirls into negation and back into fire and ashes. For I am the Captain of the undead! I am the son of Nyankonpon! I am the child of Sasabonsam! I am the breed of the Lord of Hell, the breath of Ezekiel, the blood of Ezekiel and the Bones made Holy and whole with the blessings of Abysina Clarissa.*

PRAYER:

Great Black Lord of the silken trees, I call you forth from the leaves of the forest and deep dark woods! By your very name, Sasabonsam, I scream you forth as your name has been shouted by your church through ages after ages in the desert lands of the Black Watchers. And I pray that the doors to the infernal realm will be open!

SECOND CONJURATION:

Black-eyed girl of death, I call you from the western well. Come forth by the sound of the sacred calling of OBAJIFO OKOMFO. I ask that you conjoin with the white-eyed girl of the east. Be One with the words of my wish! ENOEB NEEBO OBEAYANYI!

(He might see the spirits of dead girls coming forth from these directions, coming towards him, and then naked they enter into an erotic melting into one. The Obeahman might see her as one, partly dark, partly white, with huge eyes, one black and one white, and will take notice of what she does or says or if she gives anything to him. He will then use the words of power until sufficient powers have been raised.)

THIRD CONJURATION:

Readings from the four gospels and short honouring of the memory of the four evangelists Matthew 1:1,2, Mark 1: 2,3,6, Luke 1: 8-12, John 1: 5, 7-12 should be read and the synthesis of the four will die in the Obeahman's palm and be resurrected into Bones.

The Obeahman will then take his Obeahcane, or
Obeahbox in his hands and allow the powers evoked
to enter his cranium while sitting or standing with his
powertool between his hands. He should rapidly observe
strange sensations around the jaws and along the sides of
the cranium. He will repeat in silence: *I AM THE SON OF
BONES. HIS BLOOD IS IN MY VEINS. I AM BONES* as
many times as needed to enter into full melding with the
evoked forces.

At this point he might allow the possession to conclude
his mass, or he might consecrate a simple mass in the form
of the host and/or wine, or he can, since he at this point
is Bones, command the Zombee-King Oto into the ritual
and conclude the ritual by giving offerings to Bones and
Oto in the name of Abysina Clarissa. In this manner the
two spirits present will partake of the sacraments of Anima
Sola as the containers of the sacred powers of Obeah, in
the sense where the cadaver has been raised into its needed
points of manifestation into the One.

It is not possible to give any outlines on how this should
be done, since at this point the Obeahman's spirit would
be so attuned with Bones that he can't make any mistake.
Names are power and therefore the names are given.

RITUAL REPTILICA DE ANANSI

This ritual is important in respect of the building of the container of the journeying Obeahman, and reflects the shamanic aspect of the cult. The Obeahman will for the purpose of this ritual obtain a piece of rounded grey slate-stone.

The stone will then be inscribed with two arrows going opposite directions from left to right, then from right to left, from top to bottom and then from bottom to the top, forming a double cross or matrices composed of four arrows all together. They are to be written above each other with approx 1 cm. distance between each of them. This will from now on serve as The Obeahman's Obeahaltar in all rituals he will perform within the cult. He will then read a short blessing from the Holy Scriptures over the stone (for instance Psalm 40:1,2,) making the sign of the cross and the inverted cross on it. Then he will turn the stone and paint the image of a gross spider on it, an oval shape with eight legs, simple and black. Now he will light four candles, one black, one red, one white and one yellow, and he will pour apricot brandy on the image of the spider and say the following prayer:

Blessed be Jack Mandora, the opener of the spider's body
Blessed be Ntikuma Tackooma, the son of the Spider
Blessed be fair and wise Crookie, the spouse and
mistress of the spider's son
Come to me as I whisper silently forth the names of access
MANDORA ARODNAM MANDORA ARODNAM
MANDORA OF THE CROSSED WAYS
MANDORA AROOROO AROOROO MANDORA OF

THE JOURNEYING MAGE
OPEN THE WAYS OF WILL AND CRAFT TO PLAY IN
THE VORTEX OF BECOMING
RECOGNIZE ME AS THE KING OF SORCERY AND
TAKE MY WORD AS THE WORD OF THE MASTER
OF OBEAH – A SEAL FOR THE PASSAGE
INTO THE UNKNOWN
MANDORA ARODNAM MANDORA ARODNAM
AROOROO MANDORA, JACK MANDORA HAS
OPENED THE CROSS OF TRANSGRESSION!

Son of the spider, Ntikuma Tackooma join with Crookie
your spouse in the play of becoming
Infuse the passage into the Night with the secret keys
molded in passes, signs and words
And reveal to me the hidden secrets of Lord Anansay
by being my guide, light and torch in the
Infernal kingdom of spiderwytchery!

The Obeahman will then whisper himself into a trance using the various spellings of the Spidergod's name given at the end of this ritual text while focusing on the consecrated seal on the stone until the Obeahman's gaze is fixed and the image lingers clear in his mind. The Obeahman will then enter through the spider and into the realm of the infernal beings. When he enters he must first call upon his totem that was revealed to him in his initiation and stay with it until the joining couple Ntikuma Tackooma and Crookie are found at the secret crossroad of yellow death in the centre of the endless landscape.

ANANSY
ANASI
ANANSAY
ANASY
ANANSI
ANANSAY

CHAPTER VI

OBEAH AND THE ENSORCELMENT OF SELF

THE OLD BUILDING A FEW QUARTERS FROM THE PUMPING nightlife is and has always been in shackles. It rises like a ghost from the concrete, a towering annoyance that casts shadows over the park that is its neighbor. It was a place of shadows and bad augurs. I lived close to this building—well, close enough to see this building and the ocean from my penthouse apartment. In the landscape of Oslo, where concrete and greenwood mingles in uncanny ways, these two points were my North and my West. My South and East don't make part of this spider story.

This building in the north used to be a factory of chocolate, but the scent of chocolate had been overpowered by the scent of mold and sadness as it had been turned into a building for residents.

One night I went to the west and gave flowers, syrups and fruits to the spirit of the Ocean. A wind took shape and my thoughts drifted to the legends of Gang Gang Sara as the wind embraced me. Gang Gang Sara was blown from her African home and was transported to the village of Les Coteaux in Trinidad and Tobago. She went through the Golden Lane and found her family who had also been brought across the Atlantic by the wind. She settled down, found her man, Tom, and upon the death of her true love she decided to ascend the silk cotton tree and fly home.

Alas, to no avail. Legend tells that eating salt impaired her gifts of spirit flight. My own thoughts wandered on in the fields of love and its consequences.

Embraced by the wind I walked north and found a tavern, dirty and cheap—and I found a friend. This friend was not new, but old, and she told me stories about the old building in the north. She had met one of the residents there, an Obeahman and she said, '*If you ever go there, be careful what you think, because he reads your thoughts. It is better to think of nothing...*'

As the night went on the party grew stronger and in our midst Odin arrived. Odin was a son of drink and drugs, debauchery and nastiness. In this night he was more like his blood brother Loki than himself. Odin spoke about monkeys and he spoke rubbish. But as beer drunk must find its release he went aside and there in the room of defecation he approached, in all his insanity, a man. He gave foul words and I drenched his mouth in his own defecation... The man, the subject of insult, stretched out his hand and said: '*I greet you, brother and friend*'.

This man, clean shaven, bald and with eyes of golden honey... my friend and brother... I laughed and felt Gang Gang Sara on my shoulders as I guarded my thoughts. And then he said, '*You have been looking for us*'... which I denied, because I never looked for the building in the North. It was always there. He said, '*Let's go for a walk,*' and we walked on. We walked to the park clad in shadows and we went up in the building that used to smell of chocolate and he said as we entered his apartment, '*Sit down and drink up*'. He gave me apricot brandy and in the cup were two die. I drunk up and spit out the dice and he said, '*Welcome my brother and friend, welcome to the fires of Hell.*'

He called a spirit and off I went, just to return with Papa Bones. I was drenched in apricot brandy and carnelian was what my clutching hands where holding. In front of me I saw burning candles and the air was thick with the scent of mint and fruits. I felt like the Ocean had taken hold of me in this apartment in the North. I couldn't speak, but I could see and I could cry. I called the spirits of waters and Ocean and the more I called them, the more I saw the Devil in front of me... His black skin was turning red with blood and his eyes blazing with fire. I saw death in those eyes—I thought—but by a secret communion I found rest and peace in the turbulence of emotional winds. I saw great Leviathan and his daughters circling my feet and I saw fair goblins and sprites cling to my torso—and I saw the pit of Hell welcoming me with chains and fire...

And I saw an old cottage in the woods and I saw spirits with red eyes as I broke down in suffering and despair. At this point a fire entered my body and soul, a hell fire, and I knew the obiya was given. I opened my eyes and the cottage was a rundown fabric... I came to my senses and I saw the devil smiling—and I knew that I had been given then secrets of the North by adhering to the torment of the West... and in this way I walked out and onwards realizing that power knows no boundaries...

Because obiya is a power given, it is an awakening to a new perception, a magical perception, it is an ensorcelment of Self and Soul and that is what Obeah is about. Obeah is about your ability to make true and functional concords with the spirits that live in the matrix of creation.

The way of Obeah is 'shamanic' in the sense that we travel in the in-betweens of worlds towards them—but in doing this we also open a gate and a bridge for constant interaction in whatever world we find ourselves to be. Obeah is the crude essence of the sorcerers' craft. It is about the bond we make with the other side, benevolent and malevolent. It is about the concord and contract we make with plants and the spirit herd of Sasabonsam. It is about acceptance and eternal becoming where creation is a spider's web of possibility. The Obeahman knows by instinct the secrets of godhood and can manipulate them in accordance with the knowledge and wisdom spirit gives. And the greatest of spirits always use the silk of creation to weave the world, which is gentleness and enigma—because when you possess kumona and obiya, this can be done in a quiet joy. In this quiet joy the Obeahman knows that he— or she—can poison the world or heal the world, and in this lies responsibility and its rejection. And it is here we find the beauty of Obeah. If we work destruction or healing, this spiderweb that is the cosmic design will always be able to balance the good and the bad—what matters is that we do what we are supposed to do. This understanding is only given by living a life with spirits. Anything else is merely an error. And in this way the Obeahman walks on sheltered by the woods, and works his obiya at the moonstruck lakes where the Fates dance feverishly in celebration of life, death and the trickery that makes Fortune and the World to go 'round.

SOME REFERENCES:

Bisnauth, Dale (1996). *History of Religions in the Caribbean*. US: Africa World Press.

De Laurence, L.W. (1902). *The Great Book of the Magical Art*. US: de Laurence Co.

Houk, James, T. (1995). *Spirit, Blood and Drums*. US: Temple University Press.

Keeney, Bradford (2002). *Shakers of St. Vincent*. US: Ringing Rocks Foundation. US: New York University Press.

Morrish, Ivor (1982). *Obeah, Christ and Rastaman*. UK: James Clarke & Co.

Olmos, Margartie, F. & Paravisni-Gebert, Lizabeth (2003). *Creole Religions of the Caribbean*. US: NYU Press.

Paton, Diana & Forde, Maarit (ed.)(2012). *Obeah and Other Powers*. US: Duke University Press.

Stephen, Henri (1998). *Winti Culture*. Amsterdam: CADELA.

Lightning Source UK Ltd.
Milton Keynes UK
UKOW06n1330311017
311940UK00001B/1/P